SALMA HAYEK

MASON CREST PUBLISHERS
PHILADELPHIA

Charles Barkley
Halle Berry
Cesar Chavez
Kenny Chesney
George Clooney
Johnny Depp
Tony Dungy
Jermaine Dupri
Jennifer Garner
Kevin Garnett
John B. Herrington
Salma Hayek
Vanessa Hudgens
Samuel L. Jackson
Norah Jones
Martin Lawrence
Bruce Lee
Eva Longoria
Malcolm X
Carlos Mencia
Chuck Norris
Barack Obama
Rosa Parks
Bill Richardson
Russell Simmons
Carrie Underwood
Modern American Indian Leaders

SALMA HAYEK

BILL WINE

MASON CREST PUBLISHERS
PHILADELPHIA

ABOUT CROSS-CURRENTS

When you see this logo, turn to the Cross-Currents section at the back of the book. The Cross-Currents features explore connections between people, places, events, and ideas.

Produced by OTTN Publishing, Stockton, New Jersey

Mason Crest Publishers
370 Reed Road
Broomall, PA 19008
www.masoncrest.com

First printing

1 3 5 7 9 8 6 4 2

Library of Congress Cataloging-in-Publication Data

Wine, Bill.
Salma Hayek / Bill Wine.
p. cm. — (Sharing the American dream)
ISBN 978-1-4222-0585-3 (hardcover) — ISBN 978-1-4222-0748-2 (pbk.)
1. Hayek, Salma, 1968—-Juvenile literature. 2. Motion picture actors and actresses—Mexico—Biography—Juvenile literature. 3. Television actors and actresses—Mexico—Biography—Juvenile literature. I. Title.
PN2318.H39W56 2008
791.4302'8092—dc22

2008044275

TABLE OF CONTENTS

CHAPTER ONE

LET FRIDA RING!

It is 5:30 A.M. on January 23, 2007, in Los Angeles, California. Actress Salma Hayek stands with Sid Ganis, the president of the Academy of Motion Picture Arts and Sciences (AMPAS). They begin to read the nominations for the 79th Annual Academy Awards.

Hayek's presence there reflects how Hollywood feels about her work. Just four years earlier, Hayek had become the first Mexican nominated for an Oscar for Best Actress. She earned it for her role as artist Frida Kahlo in the 2002 film *Frida*.

Surprise Oscar Nod

Hayek received that nomination on February 11, 2003. The audience gasped when AMPAS president Frank Pierson and actress Marisa Tomei read her name. Few entertainment-industry insiders had anticipated a nomination for the Mexican actress, a relative newcomer to American films.

READ MORE

For information about the Academy of Motion Picture Arts and Sciences, as well as the annual Academy Awards, turn to page 44.

Hayek's first major U.S. movie role was in director

Salma Hayek waves to photographers as she arrives at the Kodak Theatre in Hollywood, California, for the 75th Annual Academy Awards, March 23, 2003. Salma had been nominated for an Oscar for her portrayal of artist Frida Kahlo.

Robert Rodriguez's *Desperado* in 1995, with Antonio Banderas. By 1999, though, Hayek had started a production company called Ventanarosa ("Rose-Colored Window"). Eventually she helped create several television and movie projects through that company. She was one of the producers of *Frida*, which got multiple Oscar nominations. *Frida* also made Hayek one of only three Mexican actresses ever nominated for an Academy Award. (Best Supporting Actress nominations went to Katy Jurado for the 1955 western *Broken Lance* and Adriana Barraza for the 2006 drama *Babel*.)

Frida was a biographical drama that painted two portraits on one vibrant canvas. The main subject was artist Frida Kahlo. Kahlo was a controversial Mexican painter and feminist from the early 20th century. She was born in 1907 and died in 1954. Kahlo survived a crippling bus accident. She also had serious drug and alcohol problems. In addition, she had a rocky marriage with the film's other subject, famed artist Diego Rivera. Kahlo married the womanizing Rivera twice. In interviews, Salma Hayek had often mentioned Kahlo as a dream role.

READ MORE

Diego Rivera was one of Mexico's most important—and controversial—artists. For a brief profile of the man who married Frida Kahlo twice, see page 45.

Yet *Frida* almost did not get made. Jennifer Lopez was set to star as Kahlo in another big-screen project. But once Lopez dropped out of her project, the traffic light turned fully green for *Frida*.

"What is amazing to me," Hayek told an interviewer, "is that it got done at all. What's amazing to me is that I was able to convince the studio and someone like [director] Julie Taymor to do this film and that I was able to convince all

In 2002, Salma Hayek realized her dream of portraying fellow Mexican Frida Kahlo. Seen with Salma in this still from the biopic *Frida* is costar Alfred Molina, who played Kahlo's husband, Diego Rivera.

these big superstars to play small parts with no money and no perks."

Asked how she felt about the Academy Award nominations, Hayek responded, "Very, very excited. I am very excited that [Frida has] six Oscar nominations. I am also excited . . . for Felipe Fernandez del Paso who is the production designer in the movie. He is a very old friend."

Accomplished Ensemble

Frida had a whole cast of great performers. Alfred Molina played Diego Rivera. Ashley Judd, Antonio Banderas, Geoffrey Rush, and Diego Luna all had roles. The cast also included Edward Norton, with whom Hayek had a four-year-long romantic relationship.

But the AMPAS members were most impressed with Hayek's performance. Hayek's image instantly changed. "Salma Hayek's casting as Frida was inspired," critic Tiffany Bradford wrote in the online publication *DVD Times*. "The physical resemblance is there, but up until then, she had only a mediocre acting career and the film's success depended entirely on her performance—she did not disappoint. She was able to shift effortlessly between betrayed wife, proud artist . . . and loving daughter and sister, but her biggest challenge was in depicting the horrible physical pain Frida suffered most of her life."

Salma Hayek told an interviewer that Frida Kahlo's courageousness had been an inspiration to her since she was a young teen. "Of all the things that she was brave about I admire most her courage to be unique," Hayek said.

> Her paintings were not liked by many. She never changed her style whether people liked them or not. She had quite an unconventional relationship with Diego and I am sure people thought he was not the best thing. She did everything in life her own way.
>
> The way she dressed, cooked—everything about her was unique. She didn't care about what anybody thought and never apologized for who she was. On the contrary, she celebrated some of the things that made her different.

That description could apply to Salma Hayek herself. Her drive to do things her own way has helped make many of her dreams come true.

CHAPTER TWO

GROWING UP IN MEXICO

Salma Valgarma Hayek-Jiménez was born on September 2, 1966. Her father, Sami Hayek, was an oil company executive of Lebanese descent. Her mother, Diana Jiménez, was a former opera singer and teacher. Salma and her younger brother, Sami, grew up in Coatzacoalcos, Mexico.

The Hayeks were a well-off family, and Salma has mostly good memories of her childhood in Coatzacoalcos, an industrial city and port located along the Gulf of Mexico in the state of Veracruz. But there were drawbacks. For example, chemical spills were frequent, and the local beaches often had to be closed. When this happened, Salma liked to go to the movies or watch television.

READ MORE

For more information about Coatzacoalcos, Salma Hayek's hometown, turn to page 46.

Mischievous Pranks

At 12, Salma left her devoutly Catholic home for a boarding school in the United States. The Academy of the Sacred Heart was located in Grand Coteau, Louisiana. She took gymnastics and hoped to be an Olympic athlete.

Salma and her mother, 2006. Diana Jiménez had been an opera singer before marrying Salma's father, Sami Hayek.

Salma was both studious and religious. She was also mischievous and liked to play pranks. The nuns who ran the school asked her to leave after two years. Salma returned to Mexico, not having learned much English.

Her parents sent her to Houston, Texas, after she had finished high school. "I was 16. I got out of high school way too early," she told the *Houston Chronicle,* "and my mom didn't want me to go to college yet because she was afraid of college boys. So she sent me here with my aunt for a couple of months until my birthday. I was here for four months."

Later Salma moved to Mexico City to attend the Universidad Iberoamericana. She studied international relations and drama, but dropped out before graduating. She wanted to pursue her dream of being an actress. However, she was afraid her physical appearance would hurt her chances. "I grew up in a world where beauty was not only tall, it was white and blonde with blue eyes," she recalled. "And I'm dark, have brown eyes and brown hair and I'm short [5 feet 2 inches]. People used to say that the short thing was a deformity. I was really upset about my height and then one day I said, 'Who decided that it's better to be tall? Am I less healthy? Am I less capable?'"

Her pursuit of a show-business career began in earnest in her late teens. Salma took minor parts at first. Later she landed a role on the prime-time Mexican miniseries *Un nuevo amanecer* (A New Dawn). Overnight, it seemed, she was a celebrity.

Prime-Time Drama

In 1989, Salma Hayek appeared in the lead role of *Teresa,* a prime-time Mexican drama. She played a social climber who tries to use her beauty and charm to leave behind her poverty-stricken background.

An aerial view of Mexico City, with the Zócalo, or central square, near the middle of the photo. After graduating from high school and living for a few months in Houston, Salma Hayek moved to Mexico City to attend college at the Universidad Iberoamericana. She dropped out to pursue an acting career, however.

Teresa was very successful. Fans stopped Hayek in the street for autographs. She won Mexico's equivalent of an Emmy Award as best actress. She was a true TV star.

By most standards, Salma Hayek had made it. But not by her own standards. She was concerned that working on soap operas would create acting habits that would not help her in feature films. And she knew it was American films that Mexicans flocked to see at the local movie theaters. She was not yet in any way a movie star, which she very much yearned to be.

Back in the U.S.

That longing led Hayek to move to the United States in 1991. Though she spoke very little English, she was intent on campaigning for Hollywood stardom. "I was a very successful actress in Mexico," she revealed in the 1996 book *Toxic Fame.*

> I had a very comfortable life. I was very, very famous. I was an overnight success and I was very young. I knew that that was threatening my craft as an actress, and I left that comfortable life to come here and put my feet on the ground and work and work and work on my stuff. To get to know myself, I had to get away from all that and really dig.

She began taking acting classes in the United States. Some of the television series she received small roles in included *Street Justice, Nurses, Dream On,* and *The Sinbad Show*. She auditioned for four months for the lead in the 1993 feature film *Mi vida loca* (My Crazy Life) by writer-director Allison Anders. The role went to another actress. Still, Anders gave Hayek a one-line part so that she could get her Screen Actors Guild card. Having a SAG card would help her get other work in Hollywood. Hayek's image was also fairly prominent on the movie's poster. These were all baby steps to stardom.

The break she needed came from film director Robert Rodriguez and his wife, producer Elizabeth Avellan. Rodriguez had directed Hayek in the cable TV movie *Roadracers*. He had

Salma Hayek has worked with Robert Rodriguez on several projects. To find out more about the movie director, see page 47.

also used her as a dancer in "The Misbehavers." That was his segment of *Four Rooms*, a four-part comedy also featuring stories directed by Allison Anders, Alexandre Rockwell, and Quentin Tarantino.

Opposite Antonio Banderas

Rodriguez was directing 1995's *Desperado*, a playful shoot-'em-up that featured a barrage of bullets, bodies, bandits—and a big budget. It was a sequel of sorts to his earlier low-budget *El Mariachi*. It also featured emerging superstar Antonio Banderas as a killer/mariachi player. Rodriguez and Avellan cast Hayek opposite Banderas as his love interest, Carolina. She is a beautiful woman who owns a bookstore in a town in which nobody reads. As before, Hayek's beauty made viewers—and critics—take notice.

"Salma Hayek dresses the place up considerably," wrote critic Rita Kempley in her review of *Desperado* in the *Washington Post*, "as a sizzling senorita with the hero's best interests at heart."

The film introduced the striking actress to a much wider movie audience. And some critics did notice that something other than beauty was on display. "Popular Mexican TV star Salma Hayek plays a woman who can be every bit as lethal as El Mariachi," reviewer Marjorie Baumgarten wrote in the *Austin Chronicle*. "When first we see her, she is causing multiple car crashes by merely walking across the street. Visually, Banderas and Hayek make a stunning pair with their long dark hair framing them in a voluptuous cascade, and their

Salma Hayek got her big break in Hollywood when director Robert Rodriguez cast her opposite Antonio Banderas in the 1995 revenge drama *Desperado*. "He believed in me when no one did," Salma said of Rodriguez, with whom she has worked on several other projects.

sly humor and natural cunning finding in each other a natural fit."

Salma Hayek has never been afraid to take on unconventional roles. In *From Dusk Till Dawn*, she played vampire queen Santanico Pandemonium. Salma had to overcome her fear of snakes for the exotic dance scene shown in this still from the 1996 movie.

Vampire Queen

The next year, Rodriguez cast her again in his vampire thriller *From Dusk Till Dawn*. She appeared as vampire queen Santanico Pandemonium, dancing on a table in a four-minute tango with an albino python. She had bravely done her own stunts for director Rodriguez in *Desperado*. For this film, she initially refused to do the dance scene because of her fear of snakes. But she overcame her phobia and soldiered on in a role that was brief, but decidedly memorable.

Although she worked with Hollywood luminaries George Clooney and Quentin Tarantino in *From Dusk Till Dawn*, Hayek had played another small role. She had not yet felt the thrill of star billing. But it was another step in the right direction.

CHAPTER THREE

BREAKTHROUGH

The romantic comedy *Fools Rush In* was released in movie theaters over Valentine's Day weekend in 1997. Audiences saw Salma Hayek in the lead female role. The movie represented a stretch for Hayek's acting range and a change in her image.

Hayek was cast opposite Matthew Perry, a star of the extremely popular TV show *Friends*. Her character was a pregnant Mexican-American named Isabel Fuentes. Isabel is an aspiring photographer who hurriedly marries a Manhattan yuppie named Alex after a one-night stand. Despite the superficial premise, Hayek was playing a "girl next door" rather than the stunning bombshell she had so often been called on to portray.

The TV sitcom *Friends*, which ran from 1994 to 2004, was a favorite of fans and critics alike. For details, see page 48.

Hayek's job was to be likable—the film's heart—and to team up with Perry in a show of charm, class, chemistry, and charisma. She did all those things in a high-profile comedy that pleased its audience and held its own at the box office. This was

Salma Hayek with Matthew Perry in *Fools Rush In*. The 1997 romantic comedy examined cultural differences between Mexican and Anglo-American families.

the most commercially successful big-screen project she had appeared in so far.

Ebert's Blessing

Famed critic Roger Ebert called *Fools Rush In* "a sweet, entertaining retread of an ancient formula" in his *Chicago Sun-Times* review. He said that Hayek demonstrated a "comic zestfulness" that was the film's best feature. He also suggested that she "should stay away from merely decorative roles."

Los Angeles Times film critic Kevin Thomas went even further. He described Hayek as "radiantly beautiful," and the movie itself as "the perfect Valentine's Day release" and "a major breakthrough for its stars." Thomas added that the script of *Fools Rush In* has "real substance and perception, with Alex and Isabel emerging as individuals of depth and dimension."

San Francisco Examiner critic G. Allen Johnson described the film as being "bolstered by a fairly complete and convincing performance" by the "pretty and earthy" Salma Hayek, who "runs the gamut emotionally."

Cross-Culture Clash

The element of cross-culture clash in *Fools Rush In* was important to Hayek. It was part of why she responded so enthusiastically to the script. Although both Mexican and Anglo stereotypes are on display, overall she felt the screenplay respected Mexican culture and religion. She discussed this in an interview with the *Houston Chronicle:*

> I am extremely grateful to this country, and I have learned many, many things here. This movie gives me the opportunity to give something back to this country. To show something about where I come from, and about who I am, about my roots, that this country could use. And that is family values. Family unity. Family support.
>
> Of all the bad things we have, that is one good thing, family values.
>
> I just hope in some ways it's inspiring for the young American couples that are beginning a family. Because we are very affectionate. We are not afraid to touch, we are not afraid to show or say how much we love a member of the family.

Hayek earned an American Latino Media Arts (ALMA) nomination as Outstanding Actress in a Feature Film for her performance.

The ALMA Awards recognize positive portrayals of Latinos in the entertainment industry. To find out more, see page 49.

Some Mixed Years

After *Fools Rush In,* Hayek starred in a non-Hispanic role. In *The Hunchback,* a TV movie based on the great Victor Hugo novel *The Hunchback of Notre Dame,* she played the Gypsy Esmeralda. *The Hunchback,* which aired in 1997 on the TNT network, also featured Mandy Patinkin, Richard Harris, and Edward Atterton. Hayek and Atterton, a British actor, would be romantically involved until 1999.

Later in 1997, Hayek costarred with Russell Crowe in the small-scale, poorly received romantic comedy-drama, *Breaking Up.* The movie was based on a stage play that begins after the central couple has already broken up.

The next year, Hayek appeared alongside Ryan Phillippe, Mike Myers, and Neve Campbell in *54*. The fictional drama revolved around Studio 54, New York City's trendiest nightclub in the 1970s. Hayek played Anita Randazzo, the club's "coat check girl," who earns extra money teaching disco dancing. The summer release was not well received by the critics. Nor was another 1998 film in which Hayek starred, a romantic comedy called *The Velocity of Gary,* which was also a commercial flop.

That was not the case with *The Faculty,* which was released in late 1998. In the horror thriller, which reunited Hayek with director Robert Rodriguez, she played a school nurse. The science fiction fable concerned an alien invasion at a dilapidated high school. It performed respectably at the box office.

Salma Hayek, as the Gypsy Esmeralda, is led to the gallows in *The Hunchback*. The 1997 TV movie was based on Victor Hugo's classic novel *The Hunchback of Notre Dame*.

Next up for Salma Hayek was director Kevin Smith's controversial religious comedy, *Dogma,* released in 1999. The ensemble cast included Matt Damon, Ben Affleck, and Chris Rock. Hayek performed the role of the heavenly muse Serendipity.

Hayek's next major assignment was as the female lead in *Wild Wild West,* which was released in the summer of 1999. Based loosely on a TV series from the 1960s, *Wild Wild West* had Hayek playing the role of the mysterious Rita Escobar alongside costars Will Smith and Kevin Kline. The film was trashed by the critics.

New Chances in the New Century?

In spite of the mixed results from her recent films, Hayek's Hollywood stock had risen to the point that she was featured in four movies released in 2000. *Timecode* was an experimental drama by British director Mike Figgis. The film was shot entirely

A publicity photo from *54*. The 1998 movie, which was roundly panned by the critics, costarred (clockwise from top left) Ryan Phillippe, Salma Hayek, Mike Myers, and Neve Campbell.

on digital video with four overlapping stories all being shown at the same time.

Chain of Fools was a comedy-mystery that the *Variety* critic Gunnar Rehlin described as "a solid movie that's both amusing and entertaining." In it, Hayek portrayed a cop and former centerfold model investigating a murder. Playing opposite Steve Zahn, she also shared the screen with Jeff Goldblum and a young Elijah Wood.

Salma Hayek's stunning beauty and glamour were on full display in 1999's *Wild Wild West*.

Hayek then took on a starring role in the Spanish romantic comedy *La gran vida* (Living It Up). She played a hard-luck waitress who meets a millionaire and begins a whirlwind romance with huge obstacles to overcome. It was dubbed into English to take advantage of her new following, but the film failed to generate much interest.

Hayek appeared only quickly in her next project, and her role was not listed in the credits. But the movie opened to wide acclaim. It was nominated for an Oscar for Best Picture of 2000 and won four Oscars. The film was *Traffic,* director Steven Soderbergh's brilliant drama about the international drug trade. Despite the brevity of her role, Salma Hayek won notice from some reviewers. *Variety* critic Todd McCarthy wrote, "Salma Hayek shines . . . as the glamorous mistress of the Juarez druglord."

The next year's *Hotel* was directed by *Timecode*'s Mike Figgis. In this heavily improvised comedy, Hayek played a documentary filmmaker. The large ensemble cast also included Lucy Liu, John Malkovich, and David Schwimmer of the TV series *Friends*. But the critics were not amused and the public did not attend.

One from the Heart

Also in 2001, Hayek accepted the lead role in the Showtime television movie *In the Time of the Butterflies*. The film was inspired by the true story of three sisters who were killed in 1960 for their part in a plot to overthrow the Dominican Republic's brutal dictator, Rafael Trujillo. Hayek played Minerva Mirabal, who leads her sisters into the resistance movement against Trujillo after he has murdered their father. Edward James Olmos played the dictator.

San Francisco Chronicle TV critic John Carman assessed *In the Time of the Butterflies* as "Salma Hayek's serious movie, after all those action flicks and her coquettish turns on late-night talk shows. So serious that the Mexican actress is the film's co-producer as well as its star. This one, obviously, is from the heart." Carman also considered Hayek's Minerva the "only full-boiled character in the piece."

For her efforts, Hayek won an ALMA Award as the Outstanding Actor/Actress in a Made-for-Television Movie or Miniseries. She was also nominated for a Critics Choice Award as Best Actress in a Picture Made for Television. It would not be the last time Hayek would successfully portray a real-life character. It was also not her last return to television—or the last time she would take on the title of producer in the name of artistic fulfillment.

CHAPTER FOUR

MAKING UGLY BEAUTIFUL

When Mexican painter Frida Kahlo's art became popular again in the 1990s, interest surfaced in a movie about her life. Hollywood studios had previously turned down that idea. But the renewed interest certainly got the attention of Salma Hayek, who had long admired Kahlo and very much wanted to be part of such a project.

Luis Valdez—director of 1987's *La Bamba,* about the life of singer Ritchie Valens—was slated to direct a Frida Kahlo biopic. Hayek pitched herself for the title role but was told she was too young. In that case, Hayek replied, the producers would have to wait until she was old enough.

That is essentially what happened. Valdez's project stalled, and in the meantime Hayek demonstrated her box-office appeal with starring roles in movies such as *Desperado* and *From Dusk Till Dawn.* In 1997, Trimark Pictures bought the Kahlo script and hired Hayek to produce and star in the film.

Hayek would say that the script spoke to her heart. But bringing the story of Frida Kahlo, and her complex relationship with Diego Rivera, to the big screen would not be easy. While the movie would in some respects be a love story, it was hardly the kind of love story audiences were used to seeing. Kahlo and

A still from *Frida*. The movie, which was directed by Julie Taymor, took an unflinching look at the complicated relationship between Frida Kahlo and Diego Rivera.

Rivera's relationship was complicated and, at times, quite ugly. It was not romantic in the conventional sense.

Then there was the challenge of depicting Kahlo's physical infirmities and continual pain. Hayek decided to wear one shoe with a slightly bigger sole than the other, which naturally produced a limp. This device also helped the actress hint at her character's emotional suffering. When shooting scenes that depicted Kahlo's life going well, Hayek consciously worked to conceal the limp; when Kahlo was distressed emotionally, Hayek would give in to the limp.

High Praise

Seattle Post-Intelligencer movie critic William Arnold described *Frida* as "an unusually vivid portrait of the artist and the influences that shaped her work." He called it the best biographical drama about the "particular agony and ecstasy of an artist's career" since director Vincente Minnelli's 1956 biopic about Vincent van Gogh, *Lust for Life*. That is high praise indeed.

Arnold also had praise for the performance of Salma Hayek. The actress, he wrote, "throws herself into this dream Hispanic role with a teeth-clenching gusto . . . and she gradually makes us believe she is Kahlo."

In the wake of *Frida*'s success, Hayek enjoyed a higher profile. She was very much in demand as an actress and producer. Over the next few years, she kept quite busy with multiple projects.

Life After Frida

In 2003, Hayek's romantic relationship with Edward Norton ended. The two had been together for four years.

Hayek appeared in two Robert Rodriguez releases in 2003. Both were sequels. She contributed one of many cameo performances in *Spy Kids 3-D: Game Over.* Then she reprised her *Desperado* character, Carolina, in the overwrought and underthought *Once Upon a Time in Mexico*. This was the third part of Rodriguez's Mariachi Trilogy. Hayek starred with Antonio Banderas and Johnny Depp in a role that was somewhat more substantial, even if she did appear only in flashbacks.

The year 2003 also brought Hayek her first opportunity to step behind the camera and direct. The project was a Showtime television movie called *The Maldonado Miracle*. The religiously themed drama starred Peter Fonda. As executive producer, Hayek was nominated for a Daytime Emmy Award for Outstanding Children/Youth/Family Special. She also won a Daytime Emmy for Outstanding Directing in that genre.

By 2004, Hayek had begun a romantic relationship with actor Josh Lucas. That same year, she played the female lead in an undistinguished jewel-heist thriller, *After the Sunset,* with Pierce Brosnan and Woody Harrelson. Commercially speaking, she was at the top of her game. Considered Hollywood's highest-paid Latina actress, she earned about $20 million in film contracts in 2004 alone. However, given that she was now an Oscar-nominated actress, her work in *After the Sunset* seemed somewhat of a return to the realm of "merely decorative" roles.

In 2006, Hayek headlined three movies. She costarred with Penelope Cruz in the comic western *Bandidas*. Their characters reluctantly join forces to become celebrated bank robbers in mid-1800s Mexico. Hayek starred opposite Colin Farrell in a period romantic drama called *Ask the Dust*. She portrayed a Depression-era waitress in Los Angeles who is wounded by prejudice against Mexicans. Hayek also played a notorious murderer from the late 1940s in the based-on-real-life crime drama *Lonely Hearts*. The movie starred John Travolta and James Gandolfini as detectives on her trail. Unfortunately,

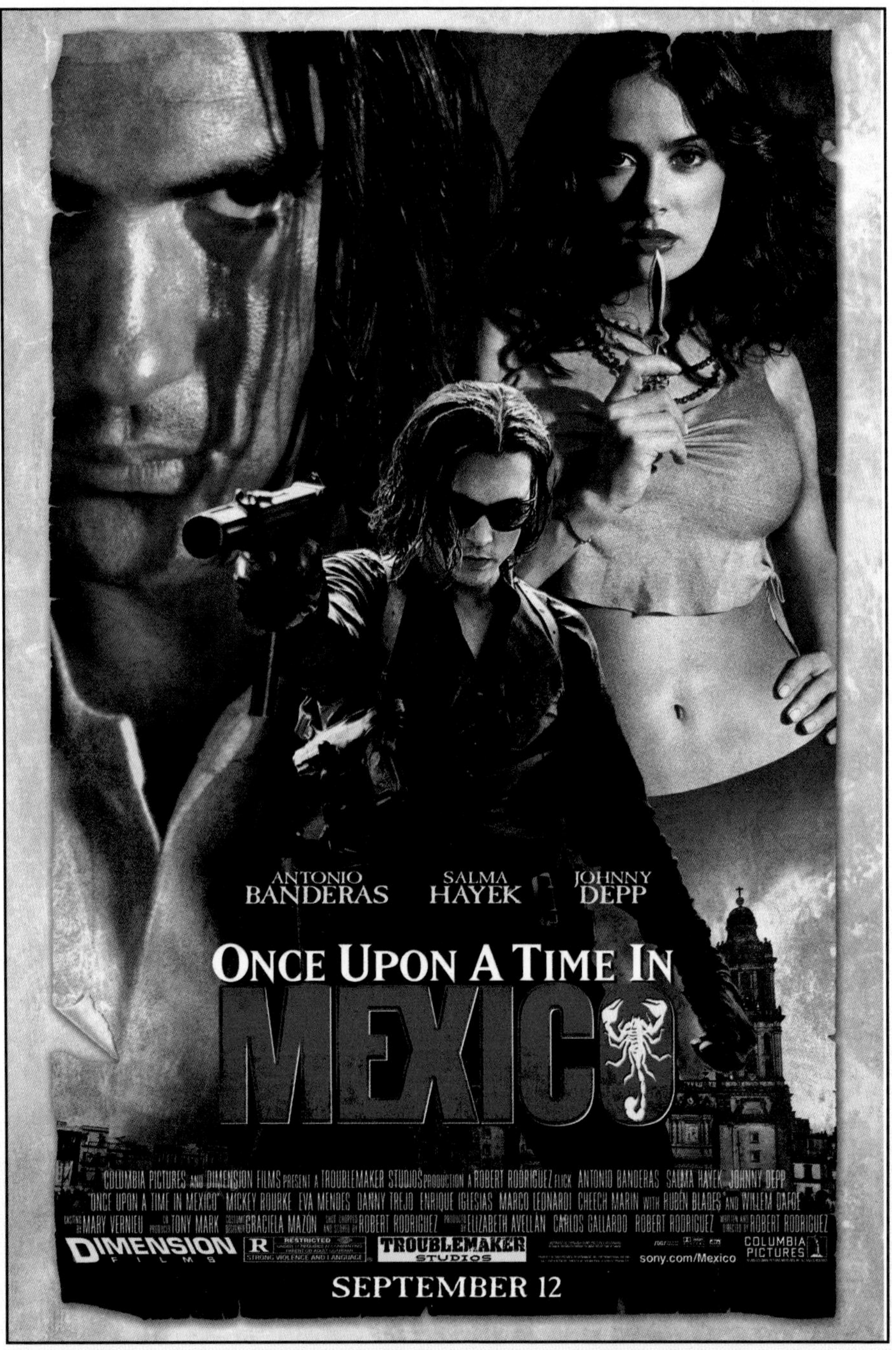

Once Upon a Time in Mexico (2003) was the third installment in director Robert Rodriguez's El Mariachi series. Salma Hayek's character, Carolina, had been killed off in 1995's *Desperado,* but she appeared in extensive flashbacks in *Once Upon a Time.*

Salma Hayek with boyfriend Josh Lucas, October 2003. The two dated for about a year.

though, none of these three films found wide theatrical release or an appreciative audience.

Turning to Betty

The project Hayek turned her attention to next, however, was a different story. Hayek became the executive producer of *Ugly Betty*. It was an adaptation of a 2001 Colombian *telenovela* (a kind of Latin American soap opera that runs for a limited time). She and co-producer Ben Silverman adapted the *telenovela*, which was called *Yo soy Betty, la fea* (I Am Betty, the Ugly Girl) for American television. The show was intended to be a half-hour situation comedy on NBC. It was later picked up by ABC and reworked as an hour-long comedy-drama. It premiered in the fall of 2006, with creator/developer Silvio Horta also producing.

READ MORE
Ugly Betty is among the entertainment projects developed by Salma Hayek's production company, Ventanarosa. For details, see page 50.

The lead character on the show is a young Latina named Betty Suarez. Betty is an unfashionable but plucky editor's assistant at a high-end New York fashion magazine. She is played by actress America Ferrera, who became well known after starring in the 2002 female-empowerment film *Real Women Have Curves*.

In addition to her work as executive producer, Hayek gave a cameo performance in the pilot episode. She has also guest-starred as magazine editor Sofia Reyes. Perhaps it is not surprising that Hayek signed on for a project that was sure to provide commentary on the appearance and exploitation of women in public and in the media.

America Ferrera and Salma Hayek in a 2006 episode of *Ugly Betty*. Salma coproduced the critically acclaimed TV series.

America Discovers America

In *Variety,* reviewer Brian Lowry lauded *Ugly Betty* and praised Ferrera's portrayal of "an ugly duckling treading water amid fashion snobs." Whatever the program's fate, he concluded, "it's going to be fun to watch America discover America."

Lowry was right. The series was an immediate hit in the United States. Within two years, versions were airing in over two dozen countries. "Bettymania" had taken hold!

The series received nominations for seven ALMA Awards in 2007. It won in four categories, including Outstanding Actress for Ferrera. It also won two Golden Globes that year, one for Best Television Series—Comedy or Musical, and one for Ferrera as Best Actress in the same genre.

Ugly Betty's most impressive showing was at the 2007 Emmy Awards. It received nominations in 11 categories—more than any other comedy series. Those nominations included Outstanding Guest Actress in a Comedy Series for Salma Hayek, as well as Outstanding Comedy Series. The show took home the Emmys for Outstanding Lead Actress in a Comedy Series (Ferrera), Outstanding Directing for a Comedy Series, and Outstanding Casting for a Comedy Series.

By the time ABC renewed the series for a third season, it was a bona fide international TV hit. Producer Salma Hayek's *Ugly Betty* had developed into a real beauty.

CHAPTER FIVE

MOTHERHOOD IN HOLLYWOOD

In March of 2007, at the age of 40, Salma Hayek made an important announcement. She was pregnant and engaged to French businessman François-Henri Pinault. Pinault was the chief executive of PPR, a company that owns the Gucci and Yves St. Laurent fashion lines as well as several French retail chains. The news was a surprise because Hayek had kept her relationship with Pinault very much a secret. Two months later, she discussed becoming a mother at 40 in an interview with *Marie Claire* magazine:

> Motherhood is not for everyone. It is for me, but there's no reason women should feel rushed to have a child. Society thinks if you don't have children, you've failed as a woman, even if you are CEO of a company. You've got to be beautiful, smart, skinny, tall, rich, successful at your job, married to the right guy—and have genius children. And by the way, you also have to be a nun!

Professionally, Hayek appeared in the film *Across the Universe* in 2007. This rock opera celebrated the music of the

A pregnant Salma Hayek with her fiancé, French businessman François-Henri Pinault, June 2007. A year later, Salma announced that she and Pinault were no longer engaged to be married.

Beatles. Hayek had a fleeting but splashy cameo in the film as a singing nurse—actually, *six* singing nurses. The project reunited Hayek with the director of *Frida,* Julie Taymor.

READ MORE

To learn about the career of director Julie Taymor, turn to page 52.

In April of 2007, Metro-Goldwyn-Mayer agreed to finance, market, and distribute Latin-themed movies under the umbrella name Ventanazul ("Blue Window"). The intent of this partnership with Salma Hayek and her production partner, José Támez, was to make English-language movies starring performers from Latin America and the United States. But something else was in the works before their company would give birth to any of their film projects.

Valentina Arrives

On September 21, 2007, Salma Hayek gave birth to a daughter, Valentina Paloma Pinault. Valentina was born at Cedars-Sinai

Salma Hayek with her daughter, Valentina Paloma Pinault, October 2008.

Medical Center in Los Angeles. But the new mother found that raising a child in the spotlight comes with a big complication: the paparazzi.

"I was hounded when I was pregnant," she explained to reporter Deborah Roberts on ABC's *20/20* in May of 2008, "and even more since I've had the baby. They are parked outside of your house and they will not move for months. I didn't leave my house for nearly three months. . . . I've gotten hit with a camera before."

READ MORE

The paparazzi are the bane of many a celebrity's existence. Page 53 has details.

When her daughter was about six months old, the protective mom clashed with photographers. In jostling to get close to Hayek for a picture, the paparazzi nearly sent little Valentina flying out of her arms and onto the pavement. "First I see them attacking me with the camera and the flashes," Hayek recalled.

> Now she starts screaming, the baby. Then they push the nanny, she was going to the floor. . . . It was so disturbing. I don't know that they wanted to get the picture or they want to push the baby and get me crazy. I'm not sure because it was almost—it was really deliberate.

Hayek screamed at the photographers and appealed to their sense of decency. But since tabloid papers will pay a lot of money for a candid photo of a celebrity mother and her baby, the paparazzi will probably never heed that kind of appeal. In part to help lessen the media frenzy surrounding her and her child,

Hayek decided to release her own photograph of Valentina. "I knew the public were curious about her, and I wanted to introduce them to my child very proudly," she said.

Raising Awareness

Hayek also had a life away from her home and the silver screen. She had worked in the past to raise people's awareness of violence against women. She had fought against the discrimination of immigrants. She also took part in the "America: A Tribute to Heroes" telethon, broadcast on September 21, 2001. It raised more than $30 million for the victims of 9/11 and their families.

The Avon Foundation and Hayek began the "Speak Out Against Domestic Violence" program in 2004. It has raised more than $7 million for organizations that combat domestic violence throughout the United States. Hayek also addressed the United States Senate about domestic violence in July 2005.

In 2006, the Harvard Foundation for Intercultural and Race Relations named Hayek "Artist of the Year." Foundation director S. Allen Counter pointed to Hayek's humanitarian work as well as her work as an actress. "She is the consummate artist, a brilliant thinker with broad intellectual interests, and a compassionate advocate for humanitarian causes," he said.

Harvard College dean Benedict Gross also lauded the work of Salma Hayek. "Because of her unique artistic talent, and humanitarian efforts in the prevention of domestic violence and breast cancer awareness, as well as her environmental advocacy, Harvard is proud to honor her accomplishments and acknowledge her fine example," Gross said.

Hayek began doing more charity work for children after the birth of her daughter in 2007. Her own charity, the Salma Hayek Foundation, was already giving support to groups

Since 2004 Salma Hayek has teamed with the cosmetics company Avon to raise awareness of, and to combat, domestic violence. Here the actress speaks out about violence against women at a 2006 press conference in Mexico City.

aiding battered women. It now also helps disadvantaged children in Mexico.

Global Initiative

When her daughter was seven months old, Hayek announced that she had joined with Pampers and UNICEF to launch the "One Pack = One Vaccine" campaign. Each package of diapers sold through the program resulted in a donation to provide tetanus vaccinations for mothers and their newborn babies in developing countries. In an interview with *People en Español,* Hayek explained that what had changed her life the most was becoming a mother. That is what led to her intense desire to help children in need:

> If you knew what it's like for kids who die from tetanus, anyone's heart would break. It's a terrible illness for these babies, because when their umbilical cords are cut, they're sealed with dirt that's completely infected with tetanus. And the worst part is that the moms don't know it. Obviously, being a mom, if I had to make one wish, it would be to have a healthy baby. Anyone can relate to that. Thinking of those poor women and kids, who have no idea how they got it and that they are infected with tetanus, makes me sad because it's unnecessary and can be solved with five cents.

Motherhood had certainly changed Hayek's priorities. And, at least for the time being, she would be raising her daughter by herself: in July 2008, she announced the end of her engagement to François-Henri Pinault. But soon Hayek would be back at work. By the end of 2008, she had five film projects in production. These included *Cirque du Freak,* a fantasy vampire thriller that was scheduled for release in 2009. Hayek starred as a bearded lady in a bizarre circus.

It was hardly the kind of role that beautiful Hollywood actresses would fight each other to get. But then, Salma Hayek has always had the courage to be unique.

Motherhood barely slowed down the hardworking Salma Hayek. Here the actress spends time with her daughter during a break in filming for *30 Rock*, October 10, 2008. Salma guest-starred on the popular TV series.

The Academy Awards

The Oscars are annual awards presented by the Academy of Motion Picture Arts and Sciences (AMPAS). Members of the Academy vote by specific categories identifying the best artists, performers, and technicians who have done the best film work over the previous calendar year.

Winners receive a 13½-inch-tall golden statuette of a man holding a sword and standing on a reel of film; the figurine is known as the Oscar. That name, according to legend, dates to 1931, when an Academy librarian is said to have exclaimed that the statuette looked like her Uncle Oscar. But the nickname wasn't officially used until 1939.

When the Academy Award ceremonies were first held in 1929, the awards represented a way of rewarding fine work and bringing respect and attention to the movie industry. During the early years, the awards were presented at small banquets in various Hollywood hotels. By the mid-1940s, the awards ceremonies were held at a series of Los Angeles theaters and auditoriums, including Grauman's Chinese Theatre and the Shrine Auditorium. Today, they are held in the Kodak Theatre in Hollywood and are broadcast to a huge international audience. The original Academy of Motion Picture Arts and Sciences had just 36 members. Today there are more than 6,500 members and voters.

The iconic Oscar on display outside Hollywood's Kodak Theatre during the 80th Annual Academy Awards, February 24, 2008.

Diego Rivera

Diego Rivera was Frida Kahlo's husband—and a world-famous Mexican painter. He is especially known for his large works in fresco, a special type of painting onto mortar or plaster walls. His work helped establish an artistic movement known as the Mexican Mural Renaissance.

Rivera was born in 1886. By the time he was 10, he was studying art at the Academy of San Carlos in Mexico City. By the early 1900s, he was traveling through Europe. He went to Italy in 1920 to study its art, including Renaissance frescoes. The next year, Rivera returned to Mexico, where he became involved in the government-sponsored Mexican mural program.

In 1922, Rivera helped begin the Revolutionary Union of Technical Workers, Painters, and Sculptors. Later that year, he joined the Mexican Communist Party as a member of its Central Committee. Major themes in his murals include traditional Mexican society, the struggle for workers' rights and social justice, and Mexico's 1910 revolution.

When Rivera married art student Frida Kahlo in 1929, he was 42 and she was 22. Neither of them was faithful, which led to a divorce in 1939. They married each other again in 1940. After Kahlo died in 1954, Rivera married Emma Hurtado, who had served as his agent for a decade. He died in 1957.

Diego Rivera, seen here with his wife Frida Kahlo, was a giant of 20th-century art. Rivera is perhaps best known for his murals.

CROSS-CURRENTS

Coatzacoalcos, Mexico

Coatzacoalcos, where Salma Hayek was born, is a city in the Mexican state of Veracruz. It is located along the coast of eastern Mexico, on the Gulf of Campeche.

During its long history, the city has had several names. It was founded as Espíritu Santo ("Holy Spirit") in 1522 by the Spanish conquistador Hernando Cortés. In 1825 the name was changed to Coatzacoalcos, which comes from an indigenous word meaning "Site of the snake" or "Where the snake hides." In 1900, the name was changed once more, to Puerto México. But since 1936 the city has been called Coatzacoalcos.

Coatzacoalcos is a major port city. With a population of more than 230,000, it ranks as the third-largest city in the state of Veracruz. Coatzalcoalcos became an important crossroads during Mexico's oil boom of the 1970s. It connects the Yucatan Peninsula and oil fields in Campeche to the rest of Mexico and to the port of Salina Cruz on the Pacific Coast. The main industry in Coatzalcoalcos is petrochemicals. Other products include sulfur and timber.

Coatzacoalcos, Salma Hayek's hometown, is a port city on the Gulf of Campeche in eastern Mexico.

The Man Behind the Mariachi

Robert Rodriguez was born and raised in San Antonio, Texas. He became an instant moviemaking legend after directing *El Mariachi,* an ultra-low-budget ($7,000) shoot-'em-up adventure film. It was a favorite at the Sundance Film Festival in 1993. *Desperado,* released in 1995, was a sequel to *El Mariachi.* Rodriguez went on to direct *From Dusk Till Dawn* (1996) and *The Faculty* (1998).

Next Rodriguez turned his attention to the family film genre. He wanted to create movies that his children could see. He made the Spy Kids trilogy: *Spy Kids* (2001), *Spy Kids 2: Island of Lost Dreams* (2002), and *Spy Kids 3-D: Game Over* (2003).

Returning to movies for grown-ups, Rodriguez directed 2003's *Once Upon a Time in Mexico,* the last film in the Mariachi trilogy. His *Sin City,* released in 2005, will result in at least two sequels.

In 2007, Rodriguez teamed up with friend and colleague Quentin Tarantino, who had costarred in *From Dusk Till Dawn,* on the double-episode film *Grindhouse.* Rodriguez directed the episode called *Planet Terror.*

Throughout his career behind the camera, Rodriguez has functioned as a one-man film crew. He often directs, produces, writes, shoots, edits, and even composes soundtrack music.

Robert Rodriguez (right), seen here with fellow director Quentin Tarantino, October 2007. The two collaborated on *Grindhouse.*

A TV Phenomenon

Friends was an award-winning television situation comedy about six friends living in New York City. It aired Thursday evenings on NBC and ran from 1994 until 2004. Since then, *Friends* has been shown in syndication and has been broadcast in more than 100 countries.

The ensemble cast included male leads Matthew Perry as Chandler, David Schwimmer as Ross, and Matt LeBlanc as Joey. The women included Jennifer Aniston as Rachel, Courteney Cox as Ross's sister Monica, and Lisa Kudrow as Phoebe. The show's success made the cast members household names. Each of them launched a movie career, with varying degrees of success.

The cast of the popular TV sitcom *Friends*, 1999. From left: David Schwimmer, Jennifer Aniston, Courtney Cox, Matthew Perry, Lisa Kudrow, Matt LeBlanc.

When the final episode of *Friends* aired on May 6, 2004, it was the fourth-most-watched finale in television series history. Only *M*A*S*H*, *Cheers*, and *Seinfeld* had more viewers for their last episodes. Over its decade-long run as a network staple, *Friends* received 63 Emmy Award nominations and won 6 Emmys. It influenced many aspects of popular culture as well, especially viewers' taste in fashion and hairstyles.

Promoting Latinos in Entertainment

In Spanish, the word *alma* means "spirit" or "soul." The ALMA (American Latino Media Arts) Awards play off that meaning. The ALMA Awards honor positive portrayals of Latinos in film and television. They have been given annually since 1995. The ALMA Awards show, held every June as a television special, brings together celebrities and leaders who influence American society. It is a celebration of Latino heritage and its positive impact on American entertainment and culture.

The ALMA Awards were created by the National Council of La Raza (NCLR). Founded in 1968, the NCLR is the largest national Latino civil rights and advocacy organization in the United States. Its mission is to improve life opportunities for Hispanic Americans. The NCLR has a network of about 300 community-based partners throughout the country. These groups provide a range of services, including job training, education, and health care.

Salma Hayek holds a 2007 ALMA Award for *Ugly Betty*. Given annually since 1995, the ALMA Awards recognize positive portrayals of Latinos in film and television.

A Rosy Window on Hollywood

As an actress, Salma Hayek has entertained audiences with her portrayals of characters ranging from a real-life artist to a heavenly muse. As a businesswoman, Hayek has helped bring acclaimed stories to movie theaters and television through her production company, Ventanarosa (which means "Rose-Colored Window").

Ventanarosa's first major film project was *El coronel no tiene quien le escriba* (No One Writes to the Colonel), a 1999 movie in which Salma Hayek also starred. The film was based on a novel of the same name by the Colombian writer Gabriel García Márquez, winner of the 1982 Nobel Prize in Literature. *El coronel no tiene quien le escriba* was Mexico's official submission for Best Foreign Film at the Oscars. It was also nominated for an award at the prestigious Cannes Film Festival. At the 2000 Sundance Film Festival director Arturo Ripstein took home the Latin America Cinema Award for *El coronel no tiene quien le escriba*.

Other projects in which Ventanarosa has been involved include the film *Frida* (2002); TV movies *In the Time of the Butterflies* (2001) and *The Maldonado Miracle* (2003); and the award-winning television series *Ugly Betty*. Clearly, Salma Hayek has become a Hollywood force to be reckoned with.

Salma Hayek's production company, Ventanarosa, brought *The Maldonado Miracle* to viewers of the cable network Showtime. Salma (second from left in this photo) also directed the 2003 film. Seen with her are (from left) Showtime president Robert Greenblatt; stars Peter Fonda, Mare Winningham, and Ruben Blades; and Showtime chairman and CEO Matt Blank.

The Golden Globes

The Golden Globe Awards, which honor outstanding work in film and television, are presented each January by the Hollywood Foreign Press Association (HFPA), whose motto is "Unity Without Discrimination of Religion or Race." The first Golden Globe Awards for achievement in film took place in 1944. In 1951, the HFPA decided to divide the best film, actor, and actress nominees into two categories: drama, and musical or comedy. This way, neither genre would be slighted. That is one way in which the Golden Globes differ from the Oscars. In 1955, the HFPA added awards for television achievement as well as film.

Current membership in the Hollywood Foreign Press Association represents 55 countries, with a combined readership of over 250 million. Publications include leading newspapers and magazines in Europe, Asia, and Latin America. All members are accredited by the Motion Picture Association of America. As the international box office has become much larger, the prestige of the Golden Globes has increased. The ceremony is now one of the most-watched award shows on television.

Jorge Camara, president of the Hollywood Foreign Press Association, at a press conference announcing the winners of the 2007 Golden Globe awards, January 14, 2008.

CROSS-CURRENTS

The Lion Queen

American theater, opera, and film director Julie Taymor is perhaps best known for her work as director of the stage version of *The Lion King* in 1997. Born in 1952 near Boston, Massachusetts, Taymor traveled and studied around the world—including in Sri Lanka, India, Paris, Japan, and Indonesia. She studied theater and puppetry and directed opera before beginning her theatrical career in New York City.

Taymor won two Tony Awards, which honor achievements on Broadway, for *The Lion King*. She dismissed the idea of completely concealing the actors who played animal characters in bodysuits and masks. Instead, she left their faces visible. This innovation helped make her the first woman to win a Tony for Best Director of a Musical.

The first feature film Taymor directed was 1999's *Titus,* an adaptation of William Shakespeare's play *Titus Andronicus*. Her 2002 film, *Frida,* received six Academy Award nominations and took home two Oscars. Taymor's experience with cross-genre and cross-cultural productions is also reflected in her 2007 film, *Across the Universe*.

Director Julie Taymor, whose film credits include *Frida* (2002) and *Across the Universe* (2007).

The Celebrity Press

The term *paparazzi* refers to photographers who relentlessly pursue opportunities to take candid photographs of celebrities as they go about their public and private lives. The word was first introduced in the 1960 film *La dolce vita* (The Sweet Life) by writer-director Federico Fellini. The movie features a news photographer named Paparazzo, played by Walter Santesso. Fellini is said to have taken the name from an Italian dialect word for a particularly noisy, buzzing mosquito.

Technological developments in cameras—including miniaturization, high-quality lenses, and high-speed films—now allow photographers to shoot their subjects from a great distance, and often without being detected. Thus, moments a celebrity might assume are private end up splashed across the pages of tabloid newspapers.

Many news agencies and publications use the term *paparazzi* to describe all photographers who take pictures of well-known people, including those photographers who are respectful of celebrities' privacy. Those who specialize in celebrity photography also claim that they are enhancing their subjects' fame. However, many people consider the behavior of more aggressive photographers to be a form of stalking. Complaints about them and their reputation as a nuisance have led to laws and curfews aimed at restricting their activities. Some people also consider their activity to be potentially dangerous. In perhaps the most famous example, paparazzi were implicated in the death of Princess Diana in a horrible car crash in 1997.

The paparazzi are the bane of many a movie star's existence.

Chronology

1966: Salma Hayek is born on September 2 in the town of Coatzacoalcos in Veracruz, Mexico.

1979: Enrolls at the Academy of the Sacred Heart boarding school in Louisiana.

1984: Enters the Universidad Iberoamericana in Mexico City to study international relations and drama.

1989: Televisa Studio in Mexico offers Hayek a television soap-opera role. She then lands the title role in the prime-time program *Teresa*.

1991: Moves to Los Angeles in pursuit of a movie career.

1993: Lands a small role in the film *Mi vida loca* (My Crazy Life).

1995: Plays the female lead opposite Antonio Banderas in the Robert Rodriguez film *Desperado*.

1997: Stars opposite Matthew Perry in the romantic comedy *Fools Rush In,* released on Valentine's Day weekend.

1999: Begins dating actor Edward Norton.

2000: Appears in four movies—*Timecode, Chain of Fools, La gran vida* (Living It Up), and *Traffic*.

2001: Coproduces and stars in the Showtime movie *In the Time of the Butterflies*.

2002: Coproduces and stars as artist Frida Kahlo in *Frida,* directed by Julie Taymor.

2003: Appears in two Robert Rodriguez films—*Spy Kids 3-D: Game Over* and *Once Upon a Time in Mexico.* Her relationship with Edward Norton ends, and she begins dating actor Josh Lucas.

2004: Partners with the Avon Foundation for the "Speak Out Against Domestic Violence" program. Her relationship with Josh Lucas ends.

2006: Stars in three movies—*Ask the Dust, Bandidas,* and *Lonely Hearts*—and signs on as the executive producer of the television series *Ugly Betty.*

2007: Contributes a cameo performance to the Julie Taymor film *Across the Universe,* announces her engagement to François-Henri Pinault, and gives birth to daughter Valentina Paloma Pinault.

2008: Joins the "One Pack = One Vaccine" campaign with Pampers and UNICEF. Ends her engagement to François-Henri Pinault.

Accomplishments/Awards

Selected Filmography

Mi vida loca (My Crazy Life) (1993)

Roadracers (1994)

Four Rooms (1995)

Desperado (1995)

From Dusk Till Dawn (1996)

Fools Rush In (1997)

The Hunchback (1997)

Breaking Up (1997)

54 (1998)

The Velocity of Gary (1998)

The Faculty (1998)

Dogma (1999)

Wild Wild West (1999)

El coronel no tiene quien le escriba (No One Writes to the Colonel) (1999)

Timecode (2000)

Chain of Fools (2000)

La gran vida (Living It Up) (2000)

Traffic (2000)

Hotel (2001)

In the Time of the Butterflies (TV; 2001)

Frida (2002)

Spy Kids 3-D: Game Over (2003)

Once Upon a Time in Mexico (2003)

The Maldonado Miracle (TV; 2003)

After the Sunset (2004)

Bandidas (2006)

Ask the Dust (2006)

Lonely Hearts (2006)

Across the Universe (2007)

Awards

ALMA Awards

1998 Nominated, Outstanding Actress in a Feature Film, *Fools Rush In* (1997)
1999 Nominated, Outstanding Actress in a Feature Film, *54* (1998)
2000 Nominated, Outstanding Actress in a Feature Film, *Wild Wild West* (1999)
2002 Won, Outstanding Actor/Actress in a Made-for-Television Movie or Miniseries, *In the Time of the Butterflies* (2001)

Critics Choice Awards

2002 Nominated, Best Actress in a Picture Made for Television, *In the Time of the Butterflies* (2001)
2003 Nominated, Best Actress, *Frida* (2002)

Daytime Emmys

2004 Won, Outstanding Directing in a Children/Youth/Family Special, *The Maldonado Miracle* (2003)

Emmys

2007 Nominated, Outstanding Comedy Series (executive producer), *Ugly Betty* (2006)
2007 Nominated, Outstanding Guest Actress in a Comedy Series, *Ugly Betty* (2006)

Golden Globes

2003 Nominated, Best Performance by an Actress in a Motion Picture—Drama, *Frida* (2002)

Oscars

2003 Nominated, Best Actress in a Leading Role, *Frida* (2002)

Screen Actors Guild Awards

2003 Nominated, Outstanding Performance by a Female Actor in a Leading Role, *Frida* (2002)

Further Reading

Dougherty, Terri. *Salma Hayek*. Farmington Hills, Mich.: Lucent Books, 2008.

Johnston, Lissa. *Frida Kahlo: Painter of Strength*. Minneapolis: Capstone Press, 2006.

Scott, Kieran. *Salma Hayek*. New York: Chelsea House, 2001.

Internet Resources

http://www.artcyclopedia.com/artists/kahlo_frida.html

A brief biography and links to artworks by Frida Kahlo, the artist featured in Salma Hayek's 2002 movie *Frida*.

http://www.imdb.com/name/nm0000161/

The Internet Movie Database's Salma Hayek page includes the actress's film, television, and production credits, as well as a short biography.

http://www.people.com/people/salma_hayek

Articles, news, biography, and photos of the actress.

Glossary

advocacy—the act of supporting or speaking out on behalf of a cause.

cameo—a very small theatrical role, often limited to a single scene, by a well-known performer.

charisma—special magnetic appeal or charm.

genre—category of artistic work, such as drama or comedy.

gusto—marked by vigor and enthusiasm.

humanitarian—relating to or done on behalf of human or social welfare, such as charity work.

improvised—made up on the spot; spontaneous.

muse—a source of inspiration.

phobia—an intense or exaggerated fear.

vaccinations—injections for the purpose of producing immunity to particular diseases.

Chapter Notes

p. 8: "What is amazing to me . . ." "Salma Hayek Interview," *View London.* http://www.viewlondon.co.uk/cinemas/salma-hayek-interview-feature-1254.html

p. 9: "Very, very excited . . ." Ibid.

p. 10: "Salma Hayek's casting as Frida . . ." Tiffany Bradford, review of *Frida,* directed by Julie Taymor, *DVD Times,* July 25, 2003. http://www.dvdtimes.co.uk/content.php? contentid=4340

p. 10: "Of all the things . . ." "Salma Hayek Interview."

p. 13: "I was 16 . . ." Louis B. Parks, "Nobody's Fool: Salma Hayek Is True to Her Mexican Roots, Family Values in Latest Hollywood Role," *Houston Chronicle,* February 13, 1997.

p. 13: "I grew up in a world . . ." PR-inside Entertainment News, "Salma Hayek Was Told She Would Never Make It in Hollywood Because Her Height Was a 'Deformity'," PR-Inside.com, April 3, 2007. http://www.pr-inside.com/entertainment-blog/2007/04/03/page/2

p. 15: "I was a very successful . . ." Joey Berlin, *Toxic Fame: Celebrities Speak on Stardom.* (Detroit: Visible Ink Press, 1996), 235.

p. 16: "Salma Hayek dresses . . ." Rita Kempley, review of *Desperado,* directed by Robert Rodriguez, *Washington Post,* August 25, 1995.

p. 16: "Popular Mexican TV star . . ." Marjorie Baumgarten, review of *Desperado,* directed by Robert Rodriguez, *Austin Chronicle,* August 25, 1995.

p. 20: "a sweet, entertaining retread . . ." Roger Ebert, review of *Fools Rush In,* directed by Andy Tennant, *Chicago Sun-Times,* February 14, 1997.

p. 20: "radiantly beautiful," Kevin Thomas, "Witty 'Fools' Produces a Romantic Rush," *Los Angeles Times,* February 14, 1997.

p. 21: "bolstered by a fairly . . ." G. Allen Johnson, "'Fools Rush In' a Respectable Offering for a Valentine's Day Love Story," *San Francisco Examiner,* February 14, 1997.

p. 21: "I am extremely grateful . . ." Parks, "Nobody's Fool."

p. 25: "a solid movie . . ." Gunnar Rehlin, review of *Chain of Fools,* directed by Pontus Löwenhielm and Patrick von Krusenstjerna, *Variety,* March 12, 2001.

p. 26: "Salma Hayek shines . . ." Todd McCarthy, review of *Traffic,* directed by Steven Soderbergh, *Variety,* December 12, 2000.

p. 26: "Salma Hayek's serious movie . . ." John Carman, "Hayek Gets Serious in 'Butterflies'," *San Francisco Chronicle,* October 19, 2001.

p. 29: "an unusually vivid portrait . . ." William Arnold, "Kahlo's Surreal World Comes Vividly to Life with Dynamic Hayek as 'Frida'," *Seattle Post-Intelligencer,* November 1, 2002.

p. 29: "particular agony . . ." Ibid.

p. 29: "throws herself into . . ." Ibid.

p. 34: "an ugly duckling . . ." Brian Lowry, "'Betty Discovers America'," *Variety,* September 24, 2006.

p. 36: "Motherhood is not for . . ." Julia Savacool, "Salma Hayek: Hot Mama!" *Marie Claire,* vol. 12, no. 5 (May 2007).

p. 39: "I was hounded when . . ." Katie Thomson, "Stars to Paparazzi: Leave Us Alone," ABC News *20/20,* May 30, 2008. http://abcnews.go.com/Entertainment/story?id=4959106&page=1

p. 39: "First I see them . . ." Ibid.

p. 40: "I knew the public . . ."

p. 40: "She is the consummate artist . . ." "Harvard Foundation Names Salma Hayek Artist of Year," *Harvard University Gazette,* February 23, 2006. http://www.news.harvard.edu/gazette/2006/02.23/03-hayek.html

p. 40: "Because of her unique . . ." Ibid.

p. 42: "If you knew what . . ." "Salma Hayek: I Learn from Valentina Every Day," Peopleenespanol.com, April 8, 2008. http://www.peopleenespanol.com/pespanol/en/articles/0,22490,1728980,00.html

Index

Numbers in ***bold italics*** refer to captions.

Photo Credits

7: Steve Granitz/WireImage/Getty Images
9: Miramax/Dimension/The Kobal Collection/Sorel, Peter
12: Steve Granitz/WireImage/Getty Images
14: Used under license from Shutterstock, Inc.
17: Columbia/The Kobal Collection/Torres, Tico
18: Los Hooligans/A Band Apart/The Kobal Collection/Podell, Joyce
20: Columbia/The Kobal Collection
23: Tri-Star TV/The Kobal Collection
24: Miramax/The Kobal Collection
25: Warner Bros/The Kobal Collection/White, Timothy
28: Miramax/Dimension/The Kobal Collection/Sorel, Peter
31: Miramax/Columbia/The Kobal Collection
32: Jeffrey Mayer/WireImage/Getty Images
34: ABC-TV/The Kobal Collection/Feld, Danny
37: Daniele Venturelli/WireImage/Getty Images
38: Arnaldo Magnani/Getty Images
41: Susana Gonzalez/AFP/Getty Images
43: Jeffrey Ufberg/WireImage/Getty Images
44: Used under license from Shutterstock, Inc.
45: Library of Congress
46: Courtesy Pure360x
47: Frank Micelotta/Getty Images
48: Getty Images
49: Jeffrey Mayer/WireImage/Getty Images
50: Frederick M. Brown/Getty Images
51: Gabriel Bouys/AFP/Getty Images
52: Bryan Bedder/Getty Images
53: Used under license from Shutterstock, Inc.

Cover Images
Main Image: Valery Hache/AFP/Getty Images
Top Inset: Kevin Winter/Getty Images
Bottom Inset: Robert Mora/Getty Images

About the Author

Bill Wine is a writer specializing in entertainment. He teaches film at La Salle University in Philadelphia and serves as the movie critic for KYW Newsradio. He lives in Wyncote, Pennsylvania, with his wife Suzanne and has two daughters, Simone and Paulina.